Wheels and Axles

by Michael Dahl

Bridgestone Books
an Imprint of Capstone Press

Bridgestone Books are published by Capstone Press
818 North Willow Street, Mankato, Minnesota 56001
Copyright © 1996 by Capstone Press
Printed in the United States of America

Library of Congress Cataloging-in-Publication Data
Dahl, Michael S.
    Wheels and axles/by Michael S. Dahl
    p. cm. -- (Early reader science. Simple machines)
    Includes bibliographical references and index.
    Summary: Describes many different kinds, uses, and benefits of wheels and axles.
    ISBN 1-56065-446-5
    1. Simple machines--Juvenile literature. 2. Wheels--Juvenile literature. 3. Axles--Juvenile
literature. [1. Wheels. 2. Axles] I. Title. II. Series
TJ147.D326 1996
621.8'11--dc20

                                            96-27771
                                            CIP
                                            AC

Photo credits
Michelle Coughlan, 16-20. FPG/Jose Luis Banus, 4. International Stock, 6;
Bob Firth, 14; Ken Frick, 10; Keith Wood, 12. Stokka Productions, cover.
Visuals Unlimited/Jeff Greenberg, 8.

Table of Contents

Words in **boldface** type in the text are defined in the Words to Know section in the back of this book.

Machines

Machines are any **tools** that help people do work. A wheel is a machine. Cars, trucks, and bicycles roll on wheels. Wheels help people travel faster and move loads farther.

Axles

Axles are the bars that go through the center of many wheels. Motorcycles and bicycles have two axles, one for each wheel. Each axle on a skateboard holds two wheels. Cars have an axle for each wheel.

Wheels Move Other Wheels

Wheels can move other wheels. Drivers use steering wheels to turn the two front wheels of their cars and trucks. Like other wheels, steering wheels spin on an axle.

Gears

A gear is a wheel with teeth along its edge. When gears are put side by side, the teeth from one gear fit between the teeth of the other gear. Inside a watch, gears of different sizes move the watch's hands.

Clockwise and Counterclockwise

Wheels turn either **clockwise** or **counterclockwise**. When gears fit together, they move in different directions. If one gear moves clockwise, the other gear moves counterclockwise.

Sprockets

A bicycle has two or more gears called **sprockets.** They are connected with a chain. Different-sized sprockets move the bicycle at different speeds. Larger sprockets turn a wheel slower but with greater force. Smaller sprockets turn a wheel faster but with less force.

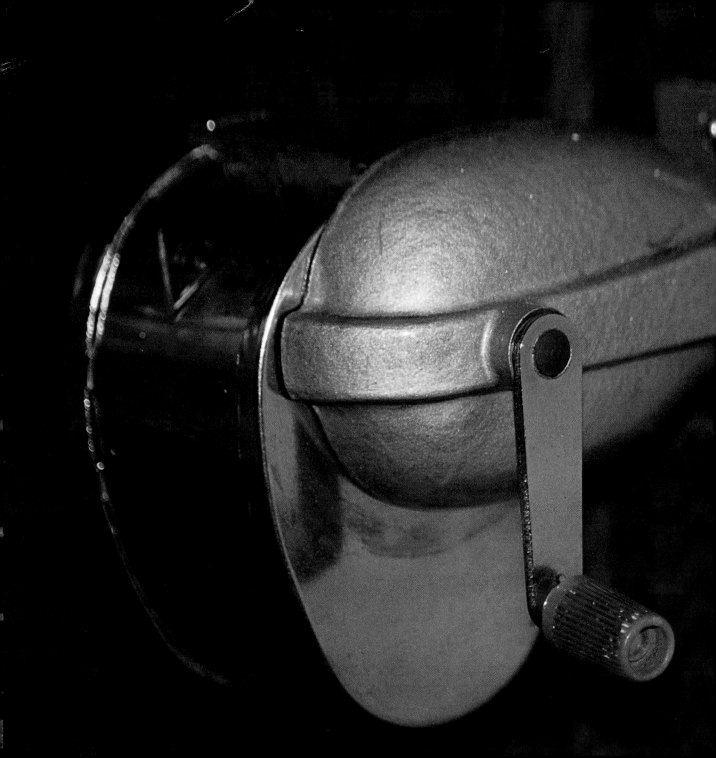

Cranks

Cranks are a kind of wheel, too. They turn around an axle and help people do work. The handle of a pencil sharpener is a crank. A bicycle pedal is a crank.

Cams

Cams are oblong wheels. They can move things back and forth or up and down. Small cams on some toys make them wobble across the floor. A **camshaft** is needed to make a car's engine run.

Wheels Work Together

An egg beater has several wheels and axles that work together. The egg beater's handle is a crank that turns a gear. This gear turns two small gears that spin the egg beater's arms. When a tool uses many simple machines together, it is called a compound machine.

Hands On: Make Your Own Wheel

Some wheels use metal balls to help them spin better. The metal balls are called bearings. They look like marbles. They are used inside the wheels of skateboards and bicycles.

What You Need

- Eight to 10 marbles
- Lids from two jars. One lid should be bigger than the other.
- Lids from pickle and peanut butter jars work best.
- A plastic plate

What You Do

1. Place the smaller lid upside down on a table.
2. Fill the lid with marbles.
3. Place the larger lid over the marbles. The larger lid should cover and almost hide the smaller lid. Make sure the marbles keep the large lid from touching the table.
4. Set the plate on the larger lid.
5. Gently spin the plate.

The plate is a wheel and so are the lids and the marbles. Since many wheels are working together, it is a compound machine. It works like the wheels of a skateboard or a bicycle. You can spin the plate either clockwise or counterclockwise.

Words to Know

camshaft—cams along an axle

clockwise—the direction in which a clock's hands move

counterclockwise—the opposite direction in which a clock's hands move

sprocket—a kind of gear with big teeth made to move a chain

tool—anything a person uses to get a job done

Read More

Ardley, Neil. *The Science Book of Machines*. New York: Harcourt Brace Jovanovich, 1992.

Berenstain, Stan and Jan Berenstain. *The Berenstain Bears' Science Fair*. New York: Random House, 1977.

Lampton, Christopher. *Marbles, Roller Skates, Doorknobs*. Brookfield, Conn.: Millbrook Press, 1991.

Rowe, Julian and Molly Perham. *Make It Move!* Chicago: Children's Press, 1993.

Index